Operation Broken Ree